My Fangs Are White and Sharp

by Jessica Rudolph

Consultants:
Christopher Kuhar, PhD
Executive Director
Cleveland Metroparks Zoo
Cleveland, Ohio

Kimberly Brenneman, PhD
National Institute for Early Education Research
Rutgers University
New Brunswick, New Jersey

BEARPORT
PUBLISHING

New York, New York

Credits

Cover, © Photoshot Holdings Ltd/Alamy; 4–5, © Michael Fogden/Photoshot; 6–7, © Daniel Gomez/NPL/Minden Pictures; 8–9, © Michael & Patricia Fogden/Corbis; 10–11, © Michael & Patricia Fogden; 12–13, © Michael Lynch/Alamy; 14–15, © Barry Mansell/NaturePL; 16–17, © Photoshot Holdings Ltd/Alamy; 18–19, © iStockphoto/Thinkstock; 20–21, © iStockphoto/Thinkstock; 22, © Barry Mansell/NaturePL; 23, © iStockphoto/Thinkstock; 24, © Joel Sartore.

Publisher: Kenn Goin
Creative Director: Spencer Brinker
Design: Debrah Kaiser
Photo Researcher: We Research Pictures, LLC.

Library of Congress Cataloging-in-Publication Data

Rudolph, Jessica.
  My fangs are white and sharp / by Jessica Rudolph.
     pages cm. — (Zoo clues)
  Includes bibliographical references and index.
  Audience: Ages 5–8.
  ISBN-13: 978-1-62724-116-8 (library binding)
  ISBN-10: 1-62724-116-7 (library binding)
  1. Vampire bats—Juvenile literature. I. Title.
  QL737.C52R83 2014
  599.4'5—dc23

                           2013036955

For more information, write to Bearport Publishing Company, Inc., 45 West 21st Street, Suite 3B, New York, New York 10010. Printed in the United States of America.

10 9 8 7 6 5 4 3 2 1

Contents

What Am I? 4

Animal Facts. 22

Where Do I Live? 23

Index .24

Read More. 24

Learn More Online 24

About the Author 24

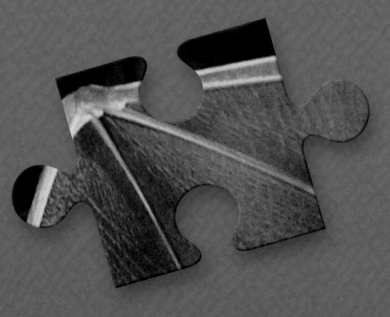

What Am I?

Look at my nose.

It is short and flat.

5

I have two feet.

Each foot has
five claws.

I have big,
pointy ears.

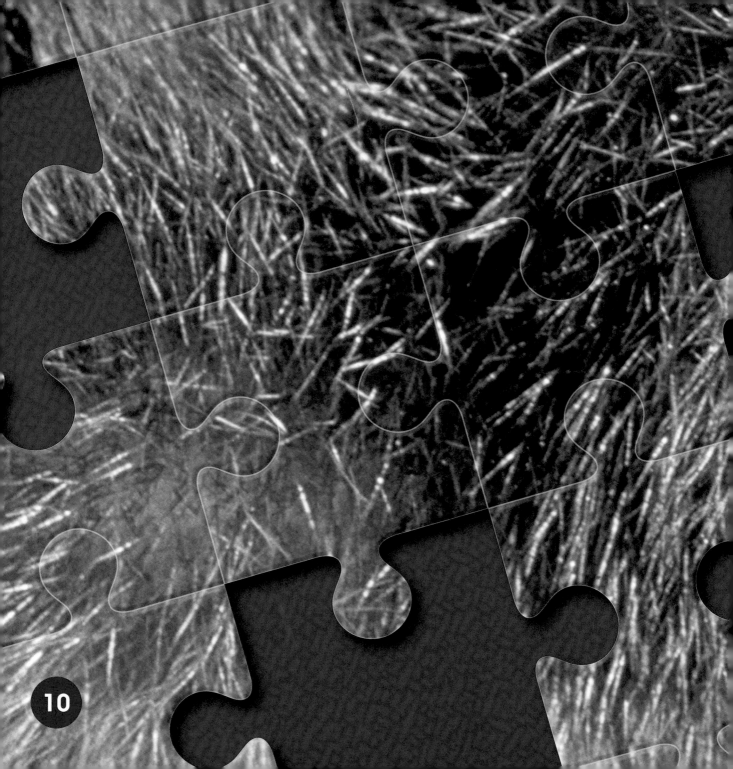

My fur is short
and brown.

I have two
long thumbs.

Each one has
a curved claw.

13

My wings are
wide.

They do not
have feathers.

My fangs are
white and sharp.

16

17

What am I?

Let's find out!

I am a
vampire bat!

21

Animal Facts

Vampire bats are mammals. Like almost all mammals, they give birth to live young. The babies drink milk from their mothers. Bats are the only mammals that can fly. Their wings are made of very thin skin.

More Vampire Bat Facts

Food:	The blood of cows, pigs, and horses
Size:	About 3.5 inches (9 cm) long, with a wingspan of 7 inches (18 cm)
Weight:	About 2 ounces (57 g)
Life Span:	About 9 years in the wild
Cool Fact:	The vampire bat doesn't suck blood. Instead, it uses its fangs to cut the skin of a sleeping animal. Then it laps up the blood with its tongue.

Adult Vampire
Bat Size

Where Do I Live?

Vampire bats live in parts of North America and South America. They make their homes in caves and other dark, hidden places.

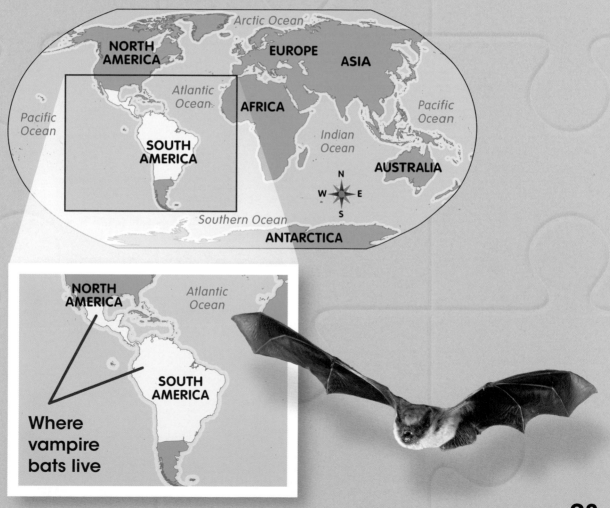

Where vampire bats live

Index

claws 6–7, 12–13
ears 8–9
fangs 16–17, 22
feet 6–7

fur 10–11
nose 4–5
thumbs 12–13
wings 14–15, 22

Read More

Carney, Elizabeth. *Bats (National Geographic Readers).* Washington, D.C.: National Geographic (2010).

Somervill, Barbara A. *Vampire Bats: Hunting for Blood (Bloodsuckers).* New York: Rosen (2008).

Learn More Online

To learn more about vampire bats, visit
www.bearportpublishing.com/ZooClues

About the Author

Jessica Rudolph lives in Connecticut. She has edited and written many books about history, science, and nature for children.